THE GREATEST
COACHES
OF ALL TIME

THE LEGENDARY WORLD OF SPORTS

BY BARRY WILNER

SportsZone
An Imprint of Abdo Publishing | abdopublishing.com

abdopublishing.com

Published by Abdo Publishing, a division of ABDO, PO Box 398166, Minneapolis, Minnesota 55439. Copyright © 2016 by Abdo Consulting Group, Inc. International copyrights reserved in all countries. No part of this book may be reproduced in any form without written permission from the publisher. SportsZone™ is a trademark and logo of Abdo Publishing.

Printed in the United States of America, North Mankato, Minnesota
082015
012016

Cover Photo: Julie Jacobson/AP Images
Interior Photos: Julie Jacobson/AP Images, 1; AP Images, 4, 7, 8, 15, 19, 45; Perry Knotts/AP Images, 10; Tom Pidgeon/AP Images, 13; Jack Thornell/AP Images, 16; Steve Simoneau/AP Images, 21; Thanassis Stavrakis/AP Images, 23; Vernon Biever/NFL Photo/AP Images, 24; Vernon Biever/AP Images, 26; Jacob Harris/AP Images, 29; Sharon Ellman/AP Images, 31; NFL Photos/AP Images, 32; Paul Spinelli/AP Images, 35; Pete Leabo/AP Images, 37, 39; Ed Bailey/AP Images, 40; Bill Kostroun/AP Images, 42

Editor: Patrick Donnelly
Series Designer: Nikki Farinella

Library of Congress Control Number: 2015945544

Cataloging-in-Publication Data
Wilner, Barry.
 The greatest coaches of all time / Barry Wilner.
  p. cm. -- (The legendary world of sports)
 ISBN 978-1-62403-989-8 (lib. bdg.)
 Includes bibliographical references and index.
 1. Coaching (Athletics)--Juvenile literature. 2. Coaches (Athletics)--Juvenile literature. 3. Sports--Juvenile literature.   I. Title.
 796.07--dc23
                                                                 2015945544

TABLE OF CONTENTS

RED AUERBACH
CELTICS CHAMPION

Arnold "Red" Auerbach was best known for two things. He won a lot of basketball games. And he celebrated those wins by lighting up a cigar on the bench.

Smoking is banned in arenas today, of course. But Auerbach was a symbol of a different era in sports. The sight of his cigar meant the Boston Celtics had won again. Auerbach coached the Celtics from 1950–51 to 1965–66. In 16 years, his teams won 795 regular-season games. Plus they won nine National Basketball Association (NBA) titles. The Celtics never had a losing season under Auerbach.

Celtics coach Red Auerbach was known as a feisty and successful leader.

His teams were built on strong defense and rebounding. They were led by center Bill Russell. He was one of the greatest defensive players in basketball history. Auerbach and Russell led Boston to a record eight straight NBA championships.

In many ways, Auerbach's worldview differed from that of his opponents. That helped make him successful as well. For example, Auerbach coached during a time when much of the country was segregated. But he was the first NBA coach to start five black players in his lineup. When he retired from coaching in 1966, he named Russell as his replacement. That made Russell the league's first black head coach.

Auerbach had a great eye for talent. The St. Louis Hawks had drafted Russell. Auerbach traded two future Hall of Fame players to get him. The move paid off for Boston. As general manager of the Celtics, he also traded for Robert Parish and drafted Larry Bird and Kevin McHale. All three players are in the Basketball Hall of Fame.

BOSTON BRUINS ALL STARS

BIRD

33

One of Red Auerbach's best moves was drafting and signing future Hall of Famer Larry Bird.

Auerbach lost his red hair long before he became a famous coach. But that is about all he lost. He joined the Basketball Hall of Fame in 1969.

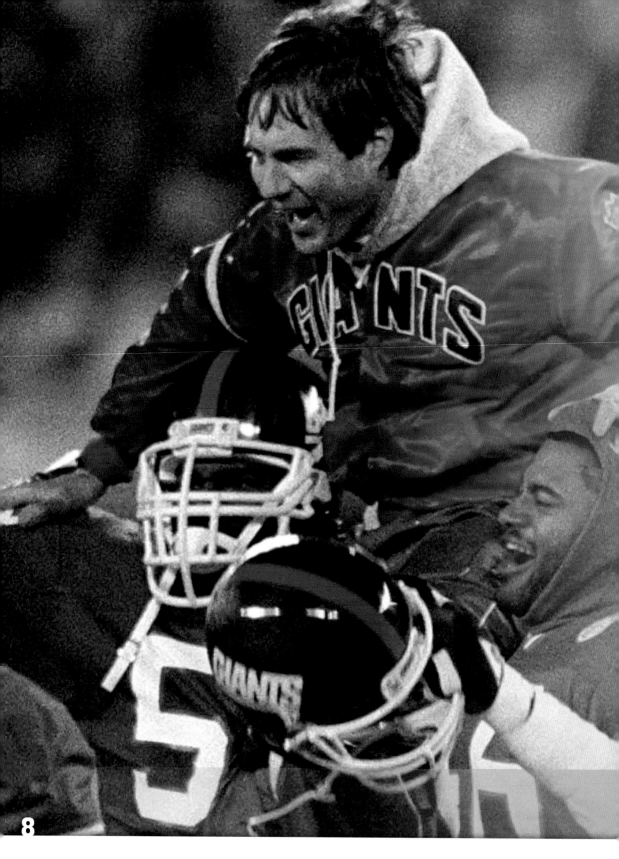

BILL BELICHICK
SUPER BOWL SUPERSTAR

Coaching is in Bill Belichick's blood. His dad, Steve, spent 33 years on the football staff at the US Naval Academy. Navy football was a big part of young Bill's childhood. He was just as interested in game plans as he was playing in games.

Belichick knew he would never be a star player. So he went into coaching at age 23. His first coaching job was as an assistant with the Baltimore Colts of the National Football League (NFL). He went on to work for three other teams. He became known as a defensive expert. The New York Giants won two Super Bowls with Belichick as their defensive coordinator. His hard

Bill Belichick was a successful assistant coach for the New York Giants in the 1980s.

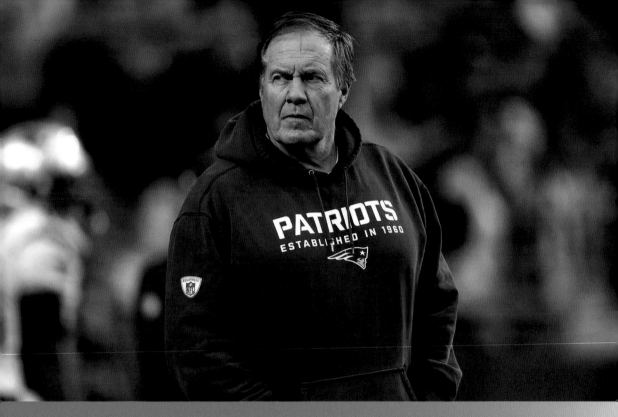

Bill Belichick's hooded sweatshirts became his signature choice for gameday attire.

work helped him land the job of head coach of the Cleveland Browns in 1991.

For the only time in his coaching career, Belichick failed. In five years, his Browns went 37–45. He was very unpopular with the Cleveland fans.

The Browns fired Belichick. So he went back to being a defensive coordinator. But he got another chance in 2000. The New England Patriots hired him as their head coach. He arrived the same year as quarterback Tom Brady. Soon the Patriots began winning. And they kept winning. By 2015 Belichick and Brady had guided the Patriots to four Super Bowl titles.

Belichick's teams usually were not flashy. Many times he let star players leave for other teams. But the new players who replaced them usually thrived. Belichick did not ask them to do too much. He put them in situations where they would be at their best. That is one mark of a great coach. Another sign? Fourteen straight years of winning records, through the 2014 season.

BUSTED!

Belichick's methods have been controversial at times. In 2007 the Patriots were caught videotaping an opponent's signals on the field. That is against the rules. The NFL fined Belichick $500,000. And the Patriots lost a high draft pick. But the Patriots kept winning. They went 16–0 that year before losing in the Super Bowl.

SCOTTY BOWMAN

STANLEY CUP COLLECTOR

Scotty Bowman won more games and more Stanley Cups than any coach in the history of the National Hockey League (NHL). But he was voted the NHL's Coach of the Year only twice in his legendary career.

Bowman won 1,244 regular-season games. He added another 223 wins and nine Stanley Cups in the postseason. But he was considered the league's best coach only in 1976–77 and 1995–96.

Not that he cared much about such awards. He was more focused on collecting championships. He won five with the Montreal Canadiens. He also won one with the Pittsburgh Penguins and three with the Detroit Red Wings.

Scotty Bowman hoists the Stanley Cup in 1997 after winning it with the Detroit Red Wings.

Bowman's first assignment in the NHL was a tough one. In 1967 the NHL expanded from six to 12 teams. The brand-new St. Louis Blues hired the 34-year-old Bowman. He took them to the Stanley Cup Finals in each of their first three seasons. They lost all three. But Bowman made an impression.

He did so well that the Canadiens—the most successful team in hockey—hired him in 1971. It was rare for a non-French-Canadian to coach in Montreal. But Canadiens fans accepted Bowman right away because he was a winner. Other coaches could worry about individual awards. Bowman won just about everything else.

PAUL BROWN
PEERLESS PIONEER

Few coaches have had a bigger impact on their sports than Paul Brown had on football. He won a lot of games as a coach and team owner. But he also changed the game.

His Cleveland Browns were the first professional team to have full-time assistant coaches. He created the first scouting system to rate college players. Brown was the first coach to call offensive plays from the sideline. He was also the first to use game film and classroom study to prepare his players to beat their opponents.

His methods were a hit at many levels. First he was a successful high school coach. Then he led Ohio State to a college national championship. Finally

Cleveland Browns players and coach Paul Brown celebrate after the team won the 1949 AAFC title game.

he founded the Browns in 1946. They played in the All-America Football Conference (AAFC). The league was a rival to the NFL. The Browns won four straight AAFC titles. Then they moved into the NFL and won the championship in 1950.

The team won two more NFL titles under Brown. But a new owner fired him after the 1962 season. That was not the end of the story, however. In 1968 Brown helped found the Cincinnati Bengals. He was their coach and owner. The Bengals became fierce rivals of the Browns. And coaches at all levels of football adopted Brown's methods.

BEAR BRYANT
AWESOME IN ALABAMA

Paul Bryant pretty much went by two names. His players called him "Coach Bryant." Everyone else simply called him "Bear."

He got the nickname because he once wrestled a bear. After doing that, how tough could coaching football be?

Bryant played college football at Alabama. Then he was an assistant coach at three schools. He also coached the sport while in the navy during World War II (1939–1945). He became head coach at Maryland in 1945 but stayed there only a year. He coached Kentucky for eight years and Texas A&M

Bear Bryant was famous for his checkered hats and for winning a lot of football games.

for four seasons. Finally, in 1958, he went back to Alabama. That is where he became a legend.

For 25 seasons Bryant and the Crimson Tide were almost unstoppable. They won six national championships, twice doing it back-to-back. Alabama went undefeated three times. It averaged more than nine wins per year under Bryant. He had a record 323 victories when he retired after the 1982 season.

Bryant was famous for wearing a checkered hat on the sideline. His players remember him more for the brutal training camps he put them through. In 1954 he took his first Texas A&M team to practice in a dusty little town called Junction, Texas. Two-thirds of the players quit before the 10-day camp ended. Bryant knew that the players who stayed were tougher than anyone they would face on the field. And two years later, the "Junction Boys" were conference champions.

Bear Bryant cut a stylish figure on the sidelines in 1957, his last year at Texas A&M.

PHIL JACKSON
THE ZEN MASTER

Phil Jackson won two NBA titles as a forward for the New York Knicks. But that whole time, he was learning on the job. His teacher was one of the sport's all-time greats, Knicks coach Red Holzman. And when Jackson became an NBA coach in 1989, he used those lessons well.

He learned so well, in fact, that he won more NBA championships than any other coach. Yes, he had a lot of help in winning those 11 titles. His teams featured superstar players such as Michael Jordan, Scottie Pippen, Shaquille O'Neal, and Kobe Bryant.

But it takes a special coach to lead such great talent. Jackson's unique philosophical approach to the game helped his players see things in new ways.

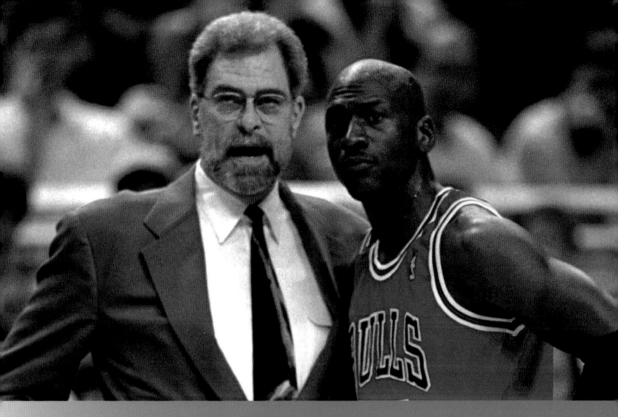

Phil Jackson, *left*, certainly benefited from coaching such superstars as Michael Jordan over the years.

And he installed an offense that allowed his star players to thrive.

Jackson won 1,155 regular-season games in 20 seasons. Plus he went 229–104 in the playoffs. Those wins include a record 11 NBA titles. He won three straight NBA crowns with the Chicago Bulls—twice. Then he did it again with the Los Angeles Lakers. He also won his last two titles with the Lakers back-to-back in 2009 and 2010.

MIKE KRZYZEWSKI
GOLD-MEDAL GREAT

NBA players began playing in the Olympics in 1992. Team USA dominated the next three Olympics. But in 2004, something unexpected happened. The star-packed US team finished third.

The national team needed a new coach. They wanted one with a history of winning. Surprisingly, a college coach emerged as the top choice. Duke's Mike Krzyzewski knew how to win. His Blue Devils teams already had won three national championships and had been to 10 Final Fours.

This, however, would be a much different challenge. Could he put together a system that worked for the pros? And would they listen to him?

Mike Krzyzewski's greatest success might be his work with the US Olympic men's basketball team.

Not to worry. In the first two Olympics under Krzyzewski, the US team did not lose a single game. They won gold medals in 2008 and 2012. Coach K found a way to get the superstars to play together. He convinced them to ignore their individual statistics. Winning was the only goal that mattered.

Meanwhile, Coach K's success in college basketball remains unmatched. In January 2015, Krzyzewski recorded his 1,000th career victory. And the Blue Devils gave Coach K his fifth national title three months later.

VINCE LOMBARDI
THE MAYOR OF TITLETOWN

Vince Lombardi was believed to have said, "Winning isn't everything. It's the only thing." He took that phrase to heart.

Lombardi's Green Bay Packers won five NFL titles in the 1960s. Among those championships were the first two Super Bowls. The Super Bowl was first played after the 1966 season. Lombardi's time atop the NFL was brief. He retired with a record of 89 wins, 29 losses, and four ties. Later he came back for one more year with the Washington Redskins. But he will be forever remembered in Green Bay. He helped the city become known as "Titletown, USA." The street outside Lambeau Field there is named after him.

Hall of Fame head coach Vince Lombardi chats with an official during a game in 1966.

Vince Lombardi, *right,* and his players shiver through the
infamous Ice Bowl game on December 31, 1967.

Lombardi was a great college lineman at Fordham.

He later was an offensive assistant with the New York

Giants. Then he took over the struggling Packers in

1959. He worked his players and coached very hard. He was not their friend; he was their boss.

In turn, they played hard—and very well.

Lombardi once said his biggest win came in Super Bowl I. The NFL champion Packers faced the Kansas City Chiefs of the rival American Football League (AFL). Everyone in the older league told Lombardi that Green Bay must win. It did, 35–10, and the Packers carried Lombardi off the field on their shoulders.

ETERNAL HONOR

Every year, the Super Bowl winner receives the Vince Lombardi Trophy. The NFL named the trophy after the coach in 1971, just four months after he died.

CONNIE MACK
BALLPARK BRILLIANCE

If you are looking for unbreakable sports records, baseball has lots of them. Start with Connie Mack. He won 3,731 games as manager of the Philadelphia Athletics. The next-closest manager is John McGraw, nearly 1,000 victories behind.

Of course, Mack also had the most losses of any manager with 3,948. That can happen when you manage for more than 50 years.

Mack was born Cornelius McGillicuddy, but he went by the shortened version of his name. He played major league ball for 11 seasons. However, he made a name for himself in the dugout. Mack helped start the American League (AL) in 1901. That same year he became part owner of the A's. For the next

Connie Mack was still managing his beloved
Philadelphia A's long past his eightieth birthday.

half-century, he was also their manager. He became
known as the "grand old gentleman of the game."
Most managers wear a baseball uniform and cap.
But Mack wore a business suit and hat. His teams won
nine AL pennants and five World Series.

In 1937 Mack was part of the second class voted
into the Baseball Hall of Fame. This happened even
though he was still managing. He continued to
manage for another 13 seasons.

URBAN MEYER
TWO-SCHOOL TITLE WINNER

Urban Meyer's teams have never had a losing record. He is more familiar with winning national titles. Meyer is the only coach to win the national championship game at two schools. He won two with Florida and another one at Ohio State.

Meyer's 2015 title with the Buckeyes was the real surprise. Ohio State was the last of four teams to make the first College Football Playoff in the 2014 season. Yet the Buckeyes shocked top-rated Alabama in the semifinals. Then they blew out Oregon to walk off with the crown.

Meyer's first head coaching job was at Bowling Green in 2001. After winning 17 games there in two years, he moved to Utah. His two Utes squads went a

Urban Meyer gets doused after his Ohio State Buckeyes defeated Oregon to win the national title.

combined 22–2. They also won the school's first major bowl game, the 2005 Fiesta Bowl. Then Meyer moved on to Florida. The Gators were 65–15 under Meyer, including 5–1 in bowl games.

All of the time and work had worn Meyer out. He stepped away from coaching in 2011. But the coaching bug bit him again a year later. The Ohio native could not turn down Ohio State. In his first three seasons in Columbus, the Buckeyes went 38–3.

DON SHULA
MIAMI MAESTRO

Don Shula was a top defensive back as a player. Then he turned to coaching. He was only 33 years old when he became head coach of the Baltimore Colts. The next year the Colts reached the 1964 NFL championship game before falling to Cleveland.

Four years later, the Colts stormed through the NFL. In the playoffs, they beat the Cleveland Browns 34–0. That set up a Super Bowl meeting with the AFL champion New York Jets. The Colts were 18-point favorites. But things did not go according to script that day.

Miami Dolphins coach Don Shula, *center*, celebrates with his players after a 1971 playoff victory in Kansas City.

"I guess I started off my Super Bowl [career] the wrong way," Shula said of the Colts' shocking 16–7 loss.

His career—Super Bowl and otherwise—turned out just fine, however. Shula left Baltimore for Miami. His Dolphins were a success thanks to a power running game and solid defense. But they lost the Super Bowl after the 1971 season.

In 1972 Shula and the Dolphins made history. They went 14–0 in the regular season. Then they won two playoff games. Finally they beat the Washington Redskins in the Super Bowl. Through 2015 they remain the only Super Bowl champion with a perfect record. The Dolphins finally lost a game the next year. But they also won their second straight Super Bowl.

Shula stayed on the Dolphins' sideline until 1995. He won 328 regular season games as a head coach. That was more than anybody in NFL history. His teams also won 16 division titles and six conference or league championships in his 33-year career.

Over the course of his 33-year career, Don Shula won more games than any coach in NFL history.

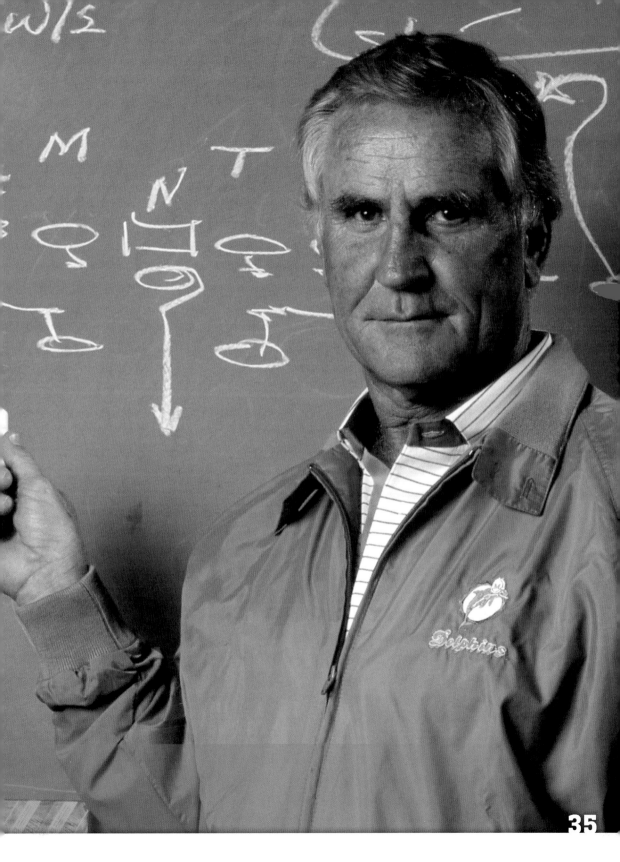

DEAN SMITH
CAROLINA'S COACH

In North Carolina, basketball is a big deal. The North Carolina Tar Heels are as famous as rock stars in that state. For 36 years, Dean Smith was the leader of the band.

Smith's teams won 879 games and two national championships. The Tar Heels reached the Final Four nine other times. Smith was known as one of the top coaches and teachers of the sport. Like a father, he kept in touch with his players after they left Carolina.

Smith could adapt his coaching style to fit his talent. North Carolina teams could win in high-scoring shootouts and tight defensive battles. His most famous contribution to the game was the four corners offense. Smith would put a player in each corner of the

North Carolina coach Dean Smith cuts down the net after his Tar Heels defeated Georgetown in the championship game of the 1982 NCAA Tournament.

offensive zone and then have the point guard dribble while looking for the perfect shot.

Most of the time, the Tar Heels found that shot, then made it. It is no wonder the school named its basketball arena the Dean E. Smith Center.

TITAN OF TENNESSEE

Pat Summitt was one of the biggest winners in the history of women's basketball. She won 1,098 games and eight national championships. But she became the head coach at Tennessee in 1974 almost by accident.

Summitt was a star player at Tennessee-Martin. She dreamed of playing for Team USA at the 1976 Olympics. But she hurt her knee early in her senior season.

Tennessee invited Summitt to become a teaching assistant. After the head coach left, she was offered a chance to take over the program. Summitt still had her eye on making the Olympics in two years. But

Team USA players carry coach Pat Summitt off the court after winning the gold-medal game in the 1984 Olympics.

she gladly took the job, because it kept her close to the game.

Women's sports were new to most colleges when Summitt took over. She helped show the world that women could perform at the highest levels too. From 1974 through 2012, Summitt's Tennessee teams never had a losing record. They won 16 conference championships and eight national titles. She also coached the US team to a gold medal in the 1984 Olympics. In 2000 Summitt was inducted into the Basketball Hall of Fame.

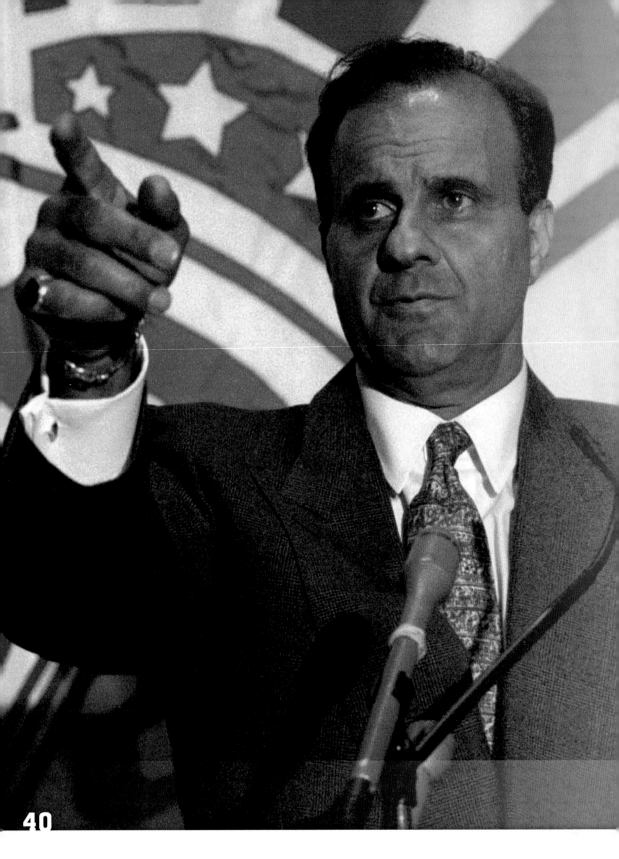

JOE TORRE
YANKEE SKIPPER

Joe Torre was born and raised in New York City. So he fit right in as a player for the Mets and manager for the Mets and Yankees.

Torre played 18 major league seasons, but he is best remembered as a manager. He led the Yankees to six AL pennants and four World Series championships.

Torre did not plan to become a manager. In 1977 he was playing for the Mets. They fired their manager 45 games into the schedule. Even though he had never managed a game, Torre took over. The Mets lost a lot. But Torre also learned a lot in his five years with the Mets. In 1982 his Atlanta Braves won the

Joe Torre took over as manager of the New York Yankees after the 1995 season and quickly made them champions.

Yankees owner George Steinbrenner, *right*, and manager Joe Torre hold the World Series trophy after New York defeated Atlanta in the 1996 Fall Classic.

National League (NL) West. But he only lasted three seasons in Atlanta. He also managed the St. Louis Cardinals for six unsuccessful years.

Torre's fortunes turned once he returned to New York. Starting in 1996, he led the Yankees to at least 92 wins in 11 of the next 12 seasons.

Torre ended his managing career with three seasons in charge of the Los Angeles Dodgers. His 2,326 wins ranked fifth in Major League Baseball history when he retired. He was inducted into the Baseball Hall of Fame in 2014.

DUAL THREAT

Joe Torre was not just a great manager. He also was a great player. He was the NL Most Valuable Player in 1971. That year he led the league in hits, runs batted in, and batting average. He made eight All-Star games and had a career .297 batting average.

JOHN WOODEN
WIZARD OF WESTWOOD

John Wooden was a native of Indiana and an All-America player at Purdue. He began making history, though, when he took the job as coach at the University of California, Los Angeles (UCLA), in 1948. There he began building the most powerful dynasty in college sports.

At that time, few top basketball players came from the West. And few were eager to head out to California to play hoops. It took many years before Wooden changed that. UCLA won its first of 10 national championships with Wooden in 1964, when it went 30–0.

That began an unmatched streak of success. The UCLA Bruins won it again in 1965 and then won seven

John Wooden wears the net around his neck after winning his record tenth NCAA championship in 1975.

straight from 1967 through 1973. Wooden coached such all-time greats as Lew Alcindor (Kareem Abdul-Jabbar), Bill Walton, Gail Goodrich, and Walt Hazzard. And they played the game simply, yet beautifully.

Wooden was the first person elected to the Basketball Hall of Fame as both a player and a coach. And the Wooden Award is given to the best male and female college basketball player each season.

HONORABLE MENTIONS

Sparky Anderson—One of two men to win the World Series with teams from both leagues (Reds and Tigers). Entered Baseball Hall of Fame in 2000.

Geno Auriemma—Led Connecticut to 10 national titles through 2015, the most for any women's college basketball coach.

Tom Landry—Guided the Dallas Cowboys for 29 seasons, winning 270 games and two Super Bowls. Entered Pro Football Hall of Fame in 1990.

Tony La Russa—The other manager to win the World Series with teams from both leagues (Athletics and Cardinals). Entered Hall of Fame in 2014.

Chuck Noll—One of two coaches (with Bill Belichick) to win four Super Bowls, leading the Pittsburgh Steelers to their first NFL title. Entered Pro Football Hall of Fame in 1993.

Joe Paterno—Won 409 games in 46 seasons at Penn State, more than any coach in major college football.

Gregg Popovich—Led San Antonio to five NBA titles in 19 seasons (1997–2015) as head coach of the Spurs.

Pat Riley—Coached the Los Angeles Lakers to four NBA titles in the 1980s, then added another with the Miami Heat in 2006.

Casey Stengel—Managed the New York Yankees to a record-tying seven World Series wins (1949–58).

Bill Walsh—Led the San Francisco 49ers to three Super Bowl wins in the 1980s. Perfected the pass-happy West Coast Offense, which spread throughout the NFL and is still popular today.

GLOSSARY

bowl game
An extra game college football teams play after the regular season.

coordinator
An assistant coach in football who is in charge of either the offense, the defense, or the special teams.

draft
The process by which leagues determine which teams can sign new players coming into the league.

dynasty
A long stretch of dominance over many years by one team.

game plan
A set of ideas or strategies a team will use against its opponent.

pennant
A flag. In baseball it symbolizes a team that has won its league championship.

segregated
Separated, usually by race or skin color.

FOR MORE INFORMATION

Books

Knapp, Fritz. *Mike Krzyzewski: Encouragement*. Chicago: Price World Publishing, 2012.

Reischel, Rob. *Green Bay Packers*. Minneapolis, MN: Abdo Publishing, 2010.

Stout, Glenn. *From Hardships to Championships*. Boston, MA: Houghton Mifflin Harcourt, 2013.

Websites

To learn more about the Legendary World of Sports, visit **booklinks.abdopublishing.com**. These links are routinely monitored and updated to provide the most current information available.

INDEX

ABOUT THE AUTHOR

Barry Wilner has been a sportswriter for the Associated Press since 1976 and has covered World Cups, Super Bowls, Olympics, and many other sporting events. He has written more than 50 books. He also teaches sports journalism at Manhattanville College, and he lives with his wife in Garnerville, New York.